Great Minds of Science

Ivan Pavlov

Exploring the Mysteries of Behavior

Barbara R. Saunders

 Enslow Publishers, Inc.
40 Industrial Road
Box 398
Berkeley Heights, NJ 07922
USA
http://www.enslow.com

Dedication
To Kenya

Library of Congress Cataloging-in-Publication Data

Saunders, Barbara R.
    Ivan Pavlov : exploring the mysteries of behavior / Barbara R. Saunders.—
    1st ed.
        p. cm. — (Great minds of science)
    Includes bibliographical references and index.
    ISBN 0-7660-2506-3
    1. Pavlov, Ivan Petrovich, 1849–1936—Juvenile literature.
    2. Physiologists—Russia (Federation)—Biography— Juvenile literature.
    I. Title. II. Series.

    QP26.P35S28 2006
    612.009— dc22

                                    2005031648

Printed in the United States of America

10 9 8 7 6 5 4 3 2 1

To Our Readers:
We have done our best to make sure all Internet Addresses in this book were active and appropriate when we went to press. However, the author and the publisher have no control over and assume no liability for the material available on those Internet sites or on other Web sites they may link to. Any comments or suggestions can be sent by e-mail to comments@enslow.com or to the address on the back cover.

Illustration Credits: B. F. Skinner Foundation, p. 75; Enslow Publishers, Inc., p. 23; Everett Collection, Inc., p. 7; The Image Works, pp. 25, 29, 56, 68, 70, 87; Jupiter Images, pp. 11, 13, 18, 39, 42, 78, 82, 88; Library of Congress, pp. 31, 46, 52, 59, 61, 64; National Archives, p. 86; National Library of Medicine, pp. 37, 72; Reproduced from the *Dictionary of American Portraits*, published by Dover Publications, Inc., in 1967, p. 49.

Cover Illustration: JupiterImages Corporation (background); Library of Congress (inset).

Contents

1

The Mastermind

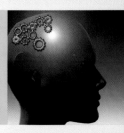

FOR MORE THAN HALF A CENTURY IVAN Pavlov pursued the scientific truth—for which he had abandoned a religious vocation. In his devotion to this cause, he changed the way people think about the relationship between their physical bodies and those experiences usually credited to their minds, hearts, and spirits. He won his highest official honor, the Nobel Prize in Physiology or Medicine, for his study of the digestive system. His greatest contribution, however, was in the realm of psychology. His work with his famous dogs suggested that the body was a complex mechanism—far more than a simple container for an otherworldly soul.

From his humble St. Petersburg laboratory, Pavlov would change the world.

Single-Minded Dedication

As a teacher at the Military Medical Academy in St. Petersburg and as a researcher at the Institute of Experimental Medicine, Ivan Pavlov was different from most of his colleagues. First, he had an unusual way of managing his laboratory. In some labs new researchers or doctors were given problems to solve on their own. This was hard work. Pavlov operated his lab more like a factory. New workers were never assigned entirely new problems at first. Instead, they repeated experimental procedures already done and written up by others. That way Pavlov got the chance to check his results many times without redoing the experiments himself or taking his senior investigators away from more advanced problems. In a way, he used his many laboratory workers as extensions of his own mind, hands, eyes, and ears.[1]

Nobel prize-winning scientist, Ivan Pavlov.

Pavlov's single-minded devotion to his quest for knowledge meant that he did not have much patience with the rules, conventions, and chores imposed by the military school he once attended. Instead, he adopted a unique, colorful style of giving lectures. He brought live animals into the classroom and demonstrated for newer students the experiments being conducted in the laboratory by senior students. Also, he used exciting, passionate words in his speeches, not the kind of words that were used in textbooks.

Another thing Pavlov was known for was his refusal to follow the school's dress code. Teachers in the Military Medical Academy, where both army and civilian doctors studied, were expected to dress in military uniforms. He did not openly defy the government, but he subtly expressed his stance that he was a scientist, not a soldier. Ivan Pavlov wore his military jacket over his street clothes. He left it unbuttoned, and did not wear the military trousers at all.[2]

Ivan Pavlov was also impatient with having to publish papers. He certainly cared about meticulously documenting the results of his experiments and those of his students. But he would rather have been carrying out experiments than grading papers or writing up his results for a publication.

When he settled in as a newly hired professor, it was the very end of the 1800s. Pavlov worked with dogs, as many of his fellow researchers did. The most common procedure for investigators was the acute experiment. A scientist would put a dog under anesthesia, operate, and let the dog die. Then he would examine the organs to try to figure out how they worked. Pavlov preferred a chronic experiment technique. He would perform surgery that would allow him to watch the organs he was studying working normally in healthy, alert animals.

Pavlov always regretted having to make animals suffer, but he felt he had to do animal experiments for the sake of humanity. Early in his career, he had been so poor that he had to live with his research dogs, so he understood that dogs have some of the same needs as human beings.

As director of the physiology laboratory at the Institute of Experimental Medicine, Pavlov demanded that his dogs be treated like human hospital patients whenever possible. Scientists and janitors kept the dogs' cages clean and used antiseptics in the operating theaters to prevent infections. Pavlov invented a special sling to keep dogs comfortable and still. Student workers were not allowed to hit dogs to get them to cooperate with procedures.[3]

Pavlov did not care much for cats, about which he ranted, "Only dire necessity can lead one to experiment on cats—on such impatient, loud, malicious animals." Pigs, he thought, were too nervous.[4]

Pavlov did not let his caring about dogs limit his scientific imagination, however. He perfected a technique for studying the digestive system of dogs. First, he would operate on a dog to make a pouch from a part of its stomach or pancreas.

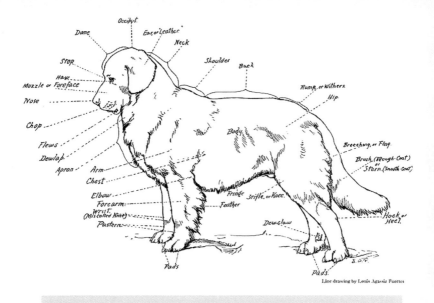

A diagram showing the external anatomy of a dog.

He was so talented with his hands that he could perform this procedure while the dog was still awake. Then, he would make a hole in a gland in its mouth and place a tube in its saliva ducts, the source of dog's drool. From these holes, called fistulas, Pavlov and his coworkers could collect juices from different parts of the dog's alimentary canal, the pathway that carries food from the mouth; through the esophagus, stomach, and intestines; and finally out of the body as waste.

In addition to allowing the dogs to eat normally from a bowl, the researchers fed the animals in a variety of strange ways—placing the food directly into their stomach pouches, or filling their mouths with chemicals that were not food at all. Sometimes they would make a hole in the dog's esophagus so that the food the dog swallowed would fall back into the bowl. The hungry dog would eat the food again and again.

Pavlov and his assistants observed that when the dog ate—even when the food never got to the stomach—the abdominal organs, including the pancreas and the stomach, would secrete their fluids. In fact, the dog produced more juice from these false feedings than it did in response to its stomach getting food that it did not see, smell, chew, or swallow. Pavlov's dogs secreted so much digestive juice that he sold some of it to doctors to give to human patients with stomach problems.

Despite the efforts to keep them healthy, most of the dogs died while these methods were still being developed and refined. A hardy dog named Druzhok, Russian for "little friend" or "pal," and another dog named Zhuchka were the first to survive long-term. Pavlov's observations of Druzhok revealed to him more than anyone had ever known about how the

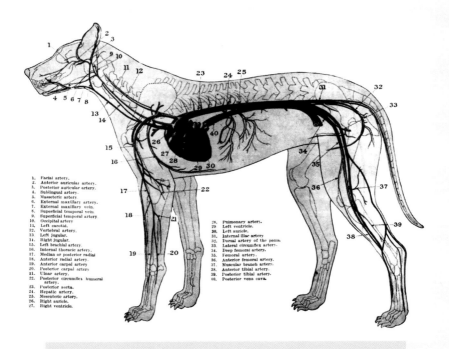

1. Facial artery.
2. Anterior auricular artery.
3. Posterior auricular artery.
4. Sublingual artery.
5. Masseteric artery.
6. External maxillary artery.
7. External maxillary vein.
8. Superficial temporal vein.
9. Superficial temporal artery.
10. Occipital artery
11. Left carotid.
12. Vertebral artery.
13. Left jugular.
14. Right jugular.
15. Left brachial artery.
16. Internal thoracic artery.
17. Median or posterior radial
18. Anterior radial artery.
19. Anterior carpal artery
20. Posterior carpal artery
21. Ulnar artery.
22. Posterior circumflex humeral artery.
23. Posterior aorta.
24. Hepatic artery.
25. Mesenteric artery.
26. Right auricle.
27. Right ventricle.

28. Pulmonary artery.
29. Left ventricle.
30. Left auricle.
31. Internal iliac artery
32. Dorsal artery of the penis.
33. Lateral circumflex artery.
34. Deep femoral artery.
35. Femoral artery.
36. Anterior femoral artery.
37. Muscular branch artery.
38. Anterior tibial artery.
39. Posterior tibial artery.
40. Posterior vena cava.

A diagram showing the internal organs of a dog.

digestive system works—in dogs or in human beings.[5]

Ivan Pavlov kept detailed records of the results of these tests. The experiments supported his concept of "nervism." The doctrine of nervism states that nerves do three kinds of jobs in every organ. The first is to signal the organ to start carrying out its function. The second is to bring chemicals through the bloodstream to the organ. The third is to regulate the rate at which those chemicals are used. Pavlov's research concentrated on the vagus nerve. It runs from the cerebral cortex of the brain, through the heart, and down as far as the colon. The vagus nerve was the topic of the thesis he wrote for his medical degree, *"The centrifugal nerves of the heart."*

A Corps of Qualified Assistants

Pavlov had new students repeat experiments he had already done to make sure his original results were accurate. These young physicians, or *praktikanty,* joined his lab hoping to quickly finish the papers they had to write to earn their medical degrees. They had the opportunity to learn a lot because Pavlov's staff of chemists and physiologists could help them understand and solve difficult scientific problems. Often, doctors who had prepared only for clinical work with patients did not have extensive training in research. The arrangement, however, benefited Pavlov as much as it benefited the students because many of them did excellent work in Pavlov's laboratory.

The Institute for Experimental Medicine charged its interns a fee. Ivan Pavlov typically arranged to have those fees waived. In return he got a steady supply of ready and able hands to help him ensure that his studies were sound.

Still, the director dreaded the time when a student's graduation thesis came due. As the supervisor of that student's project, Pavlov had to take time away from his own work to read a student's opinions and findings or to hear the student read the paper himself.

Boris Petrovich Babkin, a doctor who became Pavlov's coworker and friend, started work at the laboratory soon after he finished medical school. Dr. Babkin's previous laboratory experience had been disappointing, so he decided to become a historian of medicine. Babkin wanted to be more than just a historian; he hoped to combine his scientific knowledge with biographical and historical material. When he told Ivan Pavlov about his plan, Pavlov mocked him. "How absurd! This is utter nonsense. . . . How could such a crazy idea enter your head? Do you want to be a bookworm?"[6]

Babkin agreed to work in the laboratory, but he also kept writing. Eventually he wrote the story of Pavlov's life.

His disdain for writing almost cost Pavlov his greatest honor—the Nobel Prize. Alfred Nobel, the inventor of dynamite, established the prize to recognize people who make important contributions in science, literature, and the promotion of peace. Nobel had studied in Russia when he was a child. He was a fan of

Pavlov's and had even given money for Pavlov's laboratory.

Worldwide Acclaim

The committee of Nobel judges considered Pavlov for one of the very first prizes, in 1901. He lost. The judges liked to see the nominees publish descriptions of their discoveries in respected journals. While Pavlov lectured and wrote, he had not written as much as they expected from him. Also, his papers and lectures often gave much of the credit to work that his assistants did. Sometimes he only cited papers his students had published.

In 1904, the committee finally decided that his discoveries deserved recognition based on the findings he had published in 1897, in a book called *Lectures on the Functions of the Principal Digestive Glands*. Ivan Pavlov was granted the Nobel Prize in Physiology or Medicine. All of the past awards in that category had been awarded to professors of medicine, not to physiologists. The judges said they gave it to him "in

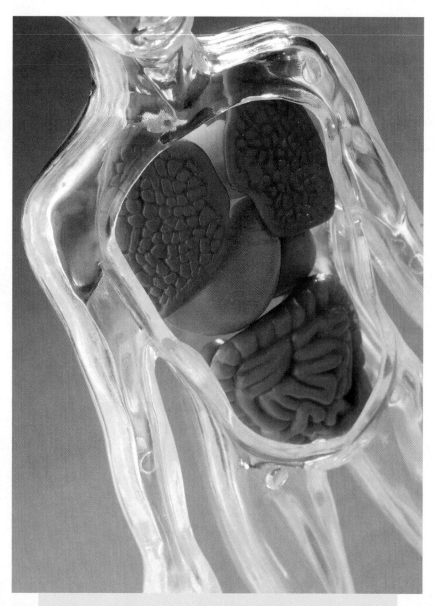

Pavlov's work contributed immensely to the understanding of human internal anatomy.

recognition of his work on the physiology of digestion, through which knowledge on vital aspects of the subject has been transformed and enlarged." [7]

He started out studying the heart and won scientific acclaim for exploring the stomach. Today, however, Pavlov is most famous for different work, work he did not begin until he was fifty years old. At the dawn of the twentieth century, he made a discovery that helped shape a new branch of medical science—psychology, the study of the mind.

Pavlov's Calling

LIKE MANY YOUNG BOYS, TEN-YEAR-OLD Ivan Pavlov expected to follow in his father's footsteps when he grew up. He would go to school at Ryazan Ecclesiastical Seminary and become a priest of the Russian Orthodox Church. He would find a wife and have children, live in a village, and work a plot of land.

A Change of Plans

By the time he was twenty-one years old, Ivan Pavlov had changed his plans: He would become a physiologist—a scientist who studies how whole organisms work. As an old man, Pavlov would say that he remained "more a peasant than a professor."[1] Pavlov never forgot the things he learned from his father, his godfather, and his life in the little town one hundred miles southeast of Moscow.

Ivan Petrovich Pavlov was born on September 14, 1849, in Ryazan, Russia. His father was Peter Dmitrievich Pavlov, parish priest of Nikola Dolgoteli. His mother was Varvara Ivanova, the daughter of a priest. Ivan was the eldest of eleven children. Ivan, Dmitri, and Peter were born within three years. Then his mother had six children who died in childhood from epidemics. The youngest two, Sergei and Lydia, survived.

The parishioners respected and admired their priest's education and position, but the Pavlovs were just as poor as the other villagers. The family made their living as peasant farmers. Even though they had little money, Peter allowed himself one luxury: He bought books. He encouraged his sons to read good books twice, to make sure that they understood them. Peter and his son Ivan shared one thing that the other family members did not. They both loved

Julian and Gregorian Calendars

- At the time Pavlov was born in 1849 and until after the Russian Revolution, Russia and other Eastern Orthodox countries followed the Julian calendar. Most European countries had been using the Gregorian calendar since 1752, the one we follow today. According to the Gregorian calendar, Pavlov's birthday was September 26.
- The events of the October Revolution took place in November according to the Gregorian calendar, which the Soviet Union adopted soon after the Revolution.

vigorous physical labor, and they regularly worked together in the orchard and garden.

A Fateful Accident

At the age of nine Ivan was seriously injured when he fell through a fence and onto pavement. His father sent him to stay with his godfather, the abbot of the monastery Saint Trinity, to recover. His godfather believed in living a simple, disciplined life filled with hard work. Godfather and godson followed an exercise regimen,

A map of Russia and its territories.

worked in the garden, ate healthful food, and read books. The boy noticed that the older man worked constantly. Sometimes when Ivan woke up in the middle of the night, he would find the abbot still at his desk.

Ivan's favorite book was *The Fables of Krylov*, which had been a gift from his godfather. He was so enthusiastic about this book that he memorized the stories in it and sometimes interrupted the abbot's work to recite one. The abbot soon established a rule: Before he could talk about a book, Ivan had to record his thoughts and impressions about it in his diary. For the rest of his life, Ivan kept the habit of carefully writing down his thoughts and observations. Later, this practice helped him keep track of his laboratory experiments.

When he was ten years old, Ivan entered the Ryazan Ecclesiastical High School. He was a year behind due to his injury and recovery period, which meant that he was in the same class as his younger brother. Both of the boys continued their education at Ryazan Ecclesiastical Seminary.

A Rapidly Changing World

It was the early 1860s and Russia was experiencing a time of uncertainty. A new ruler, Alexander II, reigned, and he was making dramatic changes. Many writers, artists, and scholars put forward grand ideas about the new kind of world that ordinary citizens should create. Many young people began to put their faith in science.

In school Ivan read about Charles Darwin's ideas about natural selection and evolution. He also read a book called *The Physiology of Common Life* by George Lewes. Ivan was very excited by Lewes's drawings and descriptions of the digestive system. So, in 1870, Pavlov left the seminary and went to the St. Petersburg University, where he entered the Faculty [School] of Natural Science. His brother Dmitri followed a year later.

The work of Charles Darwin (above) was an early influence on Ivan Pavlov.

The brothers from the village enjoyed their new life in the big city, which was the capital of Russia. When they had free time, they liked to play gorodki, a game similar to croquet. Ivan excelled at the game. He could play with either of his hands because he was ambidextrous (able to use both hands with the same ease). In his medical classes Ivan used his nimble hands to try new surgical procedures.

Ivan Pavlov, son of a priest, had found his true calling in the world of science and medicine.[2]

Studying Natural Sciences

CHARLES DARWIN CLAIMED THAT THE multitudes of different kinds of animals happen by "natural selection." Some traits help animals survive. For example, a chameleon can hide in plain sight from predators because it can change the color of its skin to match leaves, bark, or sand. Animals that have helpful traits survive in greater numbers and so produce more offspring, many of whom inherit the traits. Darwin claimed that species develop gradually by that process. He shocked and angered people who believe that God had created each unique species.

Early Influences

Dr. Ivan Sechenov, whom Pavlov credited with being "the father of Russian physiology," influenced Ivan's development as a scientist more intimately than the Englishmen Charles Darwin and George Henry Lewes did.

Sechenov's work, like Darwin's, was very controversial. Sechenov was twenty years older than Ivan Pavlov. He studied the structure and chemistry of the brain, and the role that electrical currents play in the brain's activity.

In 1863, Sechenov published his ideas in a paper called "The Reflexes of the Brain." Sechenov claimed that the brain's reflex (or automatic) responses to external events caused thoughts, feelings, and behaviors. He upset people who believed that thoughts and emotions were the product of the soul, the spirit, and the mind—nonphysical things that live inside of the body. These ideas contradicted the teachings of both religion and philosophy.[1]

Sechenov used logic and reasoning to come up with explanations for the observations made by scientists and clinical doctors. He also began to devise techniques to explore his theories in the laboratory and the classroom. Reading about

Ivan Sechenov, whom Pavlov credited as being "the father of Russian physiology."

the reflexes intrigued Ivan Pavlov and inspired him to become a physiologist. Darwin and Lewes used observation to arrive at their conclusions. Ivan Sechenov did not like to practice vivisection (experiments on live animals) himself, but he encouraged other scientists to use various kinds of experimentation to gain insight into how and why things happen in the body.

Off to Medical School

Pavlov graduated from the St. Petersburg University in 1875 and immediately began graduate studies at the Medical Surgery Academy. (Its name was changed later to the Imperial Military Medical Academy.) Ivan Sechenov, too, had studied there and stayed on as a professor until he took another job in 1870.

Pavlov soon found a teacher who believed in his talents. Ilya Cyon suggested that Ivan study the glands of the pancreas and helped his student win a gold medal for his work. Ivan planned to be Cyon's assistant at the academy, but Cyon retired before Ivan's internship began. So, Ivan took a job as the assistant of Professor Ustimovich at the Veterinary Institute. During that time he practiced and refined his skill in surgery. During a summer spent studying in Poland, he applied these skills to the study of the rabbit pancreas. He published his first paper for a scientific journal in 1878. The paper documented his research on rabbits.

From Student to Teacher

Ivan's impressive work earned him two honors. When he graduated in 1879, he received another gold medal. Also, one of his teachers recommended him in 1878 for a position in the experimental laboratory at Dr. Sergei Petrovich Botkin's prestigious medical clinic.

Dr. Botkin was known for his belief that medicine should be based on an understanding of how the body really works, not just on medical theories.

In 1875, Pavlov graduated St. Petersburg University at age twenty-six. He began graduate study in medicine immediately after.

Still, he was too busy seeing patients to supervise many experiments. So, Ivan Pavlov, fresh out of school, became the laboratory's director.

This was an ideal opportunity for the gifted, young physiologist. Until this time research science and medicine had been somewhat separate areas of expertise, with separate histories. Pavlov belonged to the new generation. He believed that the practical experience of doctors should be combined with the knowledge of scientific researchers. The next big step in Ivan Pavlov's career would be teaching at the medical school, just as Ivan Sechenov had done.[2]

The Courtship of Seraphima

BEING A DEDICATED STUDENT DID NOT keep Ivan Pavlov from doing what other young men do—going out on dates and attending parties. Ivan and Dmitri Pavlov shared an apartment in St. Petersburg, and the brothers enjoyed socializing with their friends—and with young women. Seraphima Vasilievna Karchevskaya, a student studying to become a teacher, was one of them. She was nine years younger than Ivan Pavlov.

Ivan Falls in Love

Seraphima, nicknamed Sara, was enrolled in St. Petersburg's Pedagogical Institute, a school for teachers. She was a devout Christian and a serious student of literature.

Sara was poor; her father, a captain in the Black Sea Fleet, died when she was young. Sara's mother had only her widow's pension for income. To educate and entertain herself, Sara practiced creative financing. She pawned her winter coat to pay for college one year and sold her used high school books to buy theater tickets. She tutored a younger person and split an apartment with a friend.

Sara spent her free time socializing with writers, artists, and actors. Among her acquaintances was Fyodor Dostoyevsky, who would become one of Russia's most famous writers. Dostoyevsky was known for writing about religious themes. Sara sometimes went to him with questions about her spiritual life.

Ivan was shy, and it took him a long time to approach her, but they made friends after discovering that they both loved the plays of English playwright William Shakespeare. Soon, Ivan and Sara fell in love.

Sara's family was happy with her choice of a suitor, but Pavlov's parents did not approve of

Important Places in Pavlov's Life

- When Pavlov began his studies, St. Petersburg was the capital city of Imperial Russia, as it was from 1712–1914. Its name was changed to Petrograd in 1914. In 1918, Moscow, became the capital of Russia. After Vladimir Lenin's death in 1924, Petrograd was renamed Leningrad. It became St. Petersburg again in 1991, the year the Soviet Union dissolved.
- The Institute of Physiology, which Pavlov directed after it was established in 1924, is now the I.P. Pavlov Institute of Physiology of the Russian Academy of Sciences.

the relationship. They hoped that their sons would marry wealthy girls. Ivan's behavior did not help to improve the relationship between Sara and his parents. Once, she gave Ivan some of her money for safekeeping. He spent all of it, as well as all of his own. When she asked for her money back to make a train trip, he suggested she borrow it from his parents.

Pavlov was serious about most things in his life, but he could be silly when it came to Sara.

One time, he stole one of her new shoes and kept it in his desk. She discovered it was missing only when she unpacked after a long train trip home.[1]

In 1880, Ivan Pavlov proposed. The two would spend a year apart while Sara spent time teaching school and Ivan concentrated on his medical studies. The pair wrote many love letters while they were separated. They married in 1881.

Their early life as a couple was filled with hardship. Pavlov's student stipend was not enough to support a family, leaving them to rely on Sara's sister for help. They lived with Ivan's brother Dmitri. Sara became pregnant soon after the wedding, but she lost the baby to a miscarriage.

After their son Wirchik was born, Sara took the child to go live with her family. Sara had to borrow money from Pavlov's parents to complete the grueling train ride from St. Petersburg, in the north of Russia, to Rostov-on-the-Don, in the south, a great distance. Sara was very ill by the time the trip was completed. Wirchik died

A painting of Ivan Pavlov seated at a table in his home, late in life.

several months later. Sara returned to St. Petersburg suffering from a deep depression. Her husband's mentor, Dr. Botkin, helped. He insisted that she distract herself from her misery by filling her schedule with taking walks, reading books, and bathing daily. Within a few months she got her spirit back. Sara and Ivan Pavlov eventually had four children who survived into adulthood—a daughter, Vera, and three sons, named Vladimir, Vsevolod, and Victor.

Studies Abroad

In 1883, Ivan finished his thesis *"The Centrifugal Nerves of the Heart."* He was finally a doctor of medicine. Now he was ready to continue on his path to being a scholar of physiology. Excellent performance in school earned him scholarship funding for study abroad. In 1885, he first went to Germany to study and then to Poland.

Under the direction of the famous Carl Ludwig in Leipzig, Germany, he performed surgical procedures on the heart and lungs of dogs—the organs of their cardiovascular system. This work allowed him to gain understanding of how blood pressure is maintained despite fluctuations in the state of the body. When he returned to Botkin's laboratory in 1886, Pavlov resumed his studies of the digestive system.

In 1890, Ivan Pavlov was offered a job as a professor of pharmacology at the Medical Military Academy. The same year, Prince

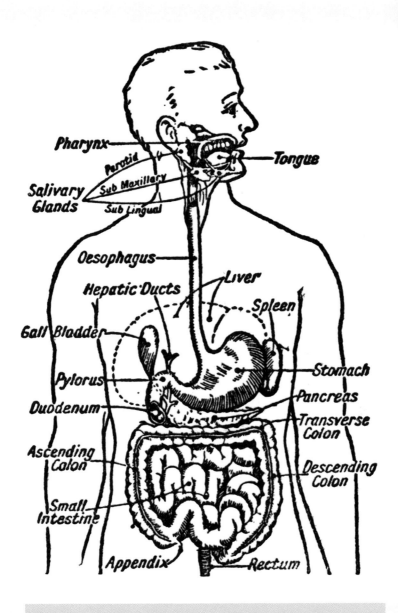

A diagram showing the major organs of the human digestive system.

Alexander Petrovich of Oldenburg established the Institute of Experimental Medicine. Ivan Pavlov was appointed Director of the Department of Physiology in 1891. For the next thirty-four years he would work at both the Military Medical Academy and the Institute of Experimental Medicine.

Married Life

Finally, Pavlov and his loyal wife could live in middle-class comfort. When he received his pay for the first time, Ivan Pavlov quickly lent almost all of the money to friends, who never paid him back. Sara, however, had learned her lesson. She managed the family's budget carefully for the rest of their married life. She had to remind Ivan each month to go to collect his salary; he resented the fact that collecting it required that he take time away from his work. Sara had a practical side that benefited her husband. She created the stability he needed at home.

Late in Pavlov's life, a writer named Lagansky shadowed him for a few weeks in order to write an article describing the famous man's daily routine:[2]

He woke early, enjoyed cups of tea and a breakfast of bread and butter, and admired his collection of Russian art. Then he went out to work. At lunchtime he took a long break for a meal and listened to records. Sometimes members of the local opera company came by to serenade the famous man during his lunch hour. When his workday was done, he came home for dinner, took a short nap, and then put in a few quiet hours in his study before retiring for the night. On Monday nights he could be found at the gym, working out with fellow members of the Physician's Athletic Society. The gym was one place where the lab workers could meet as equals. Few of these physician-athletes could beat him at gorodki.[3]

Ivan's attachment to his routine was sometimes hard on Sara. She had always dreamed of traveling to France and Italy, countries that had produced great literature. When Pavlov attained his high-level jobs, she

A modern photograph of some of Estonia's rooftops. The Pavlov family vacationed in Estonia regularly.

and her husband finally had the means to take these trips, but Pavlov was not a good travel partner. He complained about the food and the lodgings, and said these European cities were dirty compared with his beloved St. Petersburg. Eventually Pavlov insisted on embarking on his vacation on the same day each year and on going every time to the same place, Estonia.[4]

For the rest of her husband's life, Sara played the role of wife and helpmate. She brought to that role the same passion she had once applied to teaching and creative writing. Sara never completely gave up writing. She kept a record of life with her husband, with the intention of sharing it with their grandchildren. The writings became her memoirs, *Reminiscences*, published after her husband's death. Along with her letters to friends, this is one of the few sources for details about Ivan Pavlov's private life, including what he said when he learned he had won the Nobel Prize: "There is nothing exceptional in my work; it is all based on facts from which logical conclusions were drawn. That's all."[5]

The Theory of the Conditioned Reflex

HIS STUDIES ON DIGESTION AND THE Nobel Prize made him famous in Russia, but the discovery that made Ivan Pavlov most influential and gave him lasting fame began with a minor annoyance.

A Breakthrough Discovery

Pavlov's dogs, his "gastric juice factories," supplied much of the research budget at the institute. He was coming close to being able to measure exactly—to the drop—the amount of saliva and gastric juice dogs produced in response to each experimental procedure.[1]

But the researchers noticed that the dogs did not drool and secrete gastric juice only when they were fed. They did it whenever a handler walked into the room, whether or not he was carrying food they could see or smell.

Pavlov decided to investigate these "psychic secretions" to see what part they played in his theory about the nervous system. He chose to steer clear of the line of reasoning used by zoo psychologists, students of animal behavior. They said things such as, "The dog wants the food," and "The dog knows that the handler will bring food at some time." Ivan Pavlov believed that such vague, subjective statements had no place in science. He wanted to understand the physiological mechanisms that were responsible for the dogs' responses to seeing the handler. Pavlov was interested in studying not the behavior of the dog in response to a stimulus such as food, but the automatic changes in the dog's body in response to the stimulus (the reflex).

To help him better understand what he was observing, Pavlov recruited to his laboratory a few workers who had more advanced training than most of the others, including Vladimir Vulfson and A. T. Snarskii.[2] He also read the

БОЛЬШАЯ ЗАСЛУГА ПАВЛОВА В ТОМ, ЧТО ОН СОЗДАЛ МОЩНУЮ ШКОЛУ ФИЗИОЛОГОВ. ПАВЛОВ И ЕГО УЧЕНИКИ ПЕРВЫЕ В МИРЕ РЕШИЛИ ТРУДНЕЙШУЮ ПРОБЛЕМУ ЕДИНСТВА ФИЗИЧЕСКИХ И ПСИХИЧЕСКИХ ПРОЦЕССОВ

„....МЫ ПРИОБРЕЛИ ДЛЯ МОГУЧЕЙ ВЛАСТИ ФИЗИОЛОГИЧЕСКОГО ИССЛЕДО-ВАНИЯ ВМЕСТО ПОЛОВИНЧАТОГО НЕРАЗДЕЛЬНО ВЕСЬ ЖИВОТНЫЙ ОРГАНИЗМ. И ЭТО ЦЕЛИКОМ НАША, РУССКАЯ, НЕОСПОРИМАЯ ЗАСЛУГА В МИРОВОЙ НАУКЕ И ОБЩЕЧЕЛОВЕЧЕСКОЙ МЫСЛИ".

И. П. ПАВЛОВ

Старший научный сотрудник М. К. Воскресенская за работой в лаборатории Института эволюционной физиологии и патологии высшей нервной деятельности им. Павлова (Колтуши)

В МНОГОЧИСЛЕННЫХ НАУЧНЫХ ЛАБОРАТОРИЯХ СОВЕТСКИЕ УЧЕНЫЕ ПРОВОДЯТ ОПЫТЫ, ВЕДУТ ИССЛЕДОВАНИЯ, ШИРОКО ПРИМЕНЯЯ МЕТОДЫ ПАВЛОВСКОГО УЧЕНИЯ

Профессор А. О. Долин проводит опыты с собакой (Институт усовершенствования врачей в Ленинграде)

Профессор П. С. Купалов и старший научный сотрудник К. С. Абуладзе осматривают собаку после операции (Институт экспериментальной медицины в Ленинграде)

After Pavlov's many successful experiments, soon other scientists around the world began making regular test subjects of their dogs as was reported in this Russian newspaper.

writings of psychologists such as the American William James. He arrived at a tentative conclusion that his objective nature could accept: The psychic secretions are governed by the central nervous system, not by any choice or judgment on the part of the dog.

He came up with a hypothesis that he could test: The appearance of the handler somehow signals the nervous system to tell the stomach to get ready for food that is on its way.

To investigate this hypothesis, Pavlov devised a method of experimentation that his student researchers could carry out. They would engineer an association of food with some sound, sight, or smell that was neutral (neither good nor bad) to the dog and not naturally associated with food. Researchers would make a sound such as running a metronome, ringing a bell, hitting a tuning fork, blowing a whistle, or clapping their hands. Immediately afterward, they would give the dog some food.

After many repetitions of the procedure, the researcher would make the sound, but he would not feed the animal. The result of the experiment was that the animal responded to the sound by drooling and secreting stomach juices, just as if it had been fed. The chemical composition of the juices, however, was slightly different from what the animal produced when it actually ate.

Pavlov deduced that animals are predisposed to develop these associations, to help them better predict events in their environments.

Pavlov Develops a Theory

Before he could introduce his discovery to the world, Pavlov had to invent a set of terms to explain the theory he developed about reflexes. His theory said that the dogs have an "unconditional response" to food. The food is an "unconditional stimulus," something in the environment that triggers a reflexive response. Drooling in response to food happens without anyone teaching the dog to do it.

By contrast, the reflex secretion of saliva and stomach juices in response to a sound is a "conditional response." The word "conditional"

American philosopher and psychologist, William James.

(usually changed to "conditioned" when translated from Russian to English) means that the reflex happens only under certain conditions that the dog has learned to associate with the arrival of food.

Pavlov tested whether a dog could be taught to have the same response when it heard a similar—but not identical—sound. It did. That's called "stimulus generalization." He took advantage of dogs' sharp hearing to see if he could teach them that a given note from a tuning fork meant they would get food and another, slightly different, tone would not. That worked, too. He called this "stimulus discrimination."

Pavlov learned that he could also condition an animal to respond the same way by creating a second layer of "conditional stimuli." For instance, pairing the sound of a whistle with the offer of food and then pairing hand claps only with the whistle. It worked.

Then he tried presenting a conditional stimulus to a dog over and over again without giving it any food. Eventually the dog stopped responding. Pavlov called this "extinction."

As he still believed the vagus nerve was responsible for the control of the psychic secretions, Pavlov did some experiments to test what would happen if he cut it. The experiments lent some support to the theory. He found that when he cut a dog's vagus nerve, the dog would not respond normally to food or to the conditional stimuli. If he cut both branches of the vagus nerve, the dog would soon die, unable to digest its food.[3]

Bold Statements

In the fall of 1903, Pavlov shared his findings in a lecture at the Fourteenth International Medical Conference in Madrid. By the time he accepted the Nobel Prize for his advances in the study of digestion, Ivan Pavlov had decided that learning more about the subject of conditioning was much more interesting than what he had been doing.

Ivan Pavlov was already respected as a pioneer. The past winners of the Nobel Prize in Physiology or Medicine had been medical

In his Nobel speech, Pavlov made it clear that he would continue to explore new intellectual territory in the many fields of science.

doctors who had won for advances in treating disease, not physiologists. His acceptance speech made clear that he would continue to explore new intellectual territory. In the address given on December 12, 1904, Ivan Pavlov shared his aspiration to explore the conditional reflexes:

> Essentially only one thing in life interests us: our psychical constitution, the mechanism of which was and is wrapped in darkness. All human resources, art, religion, literature, philosophy and historical sciences, all of them join in bringing light in this darkness. But man has still another powerful resource: natural science with its strictly objective methods. This science, as we all know, is making huge progress every day. The facts and considerations which I have placed before you at the end of my lecture are one out of numerous attempts to employ a consistent, purely scientific method of thinking in the study of the mechanism of the highest manifestations of life in the dog, the representative of the animal kingdom that is man's best friend.[4]

6

Ivan Pavlov's Russia

The Russian Revolution

BEGINNING IN 1914, EVENTS TOOK PLACE in Ivan Pavlov's homeland that would change the course of history. Germany declared war on Russia in August 1914. This was the beginning of a war so extensive and horrible that people around the world would call it "The Great War" and "The War to End All Wars."

The name of the capital city, St. Petersburg, was changed to Petrograd in September. To some Russians the old name sounded German. The war was hard on Russian citizens. By February 1917, millions of them had died in battle. The entire population suffered under the rations the government imposed. Eventually citizens rioted in the streets of Petrograd. They felt that the tsarist government was mismanaging the war. Soldiers sent to control the crowds deserted during what came to be called the February Revolution.

On March 2, Tsar Nicolas II stepped down, and Aleksandr Kerensky became the leader of a provisional government that hoped to forge a compromise between liberals, who believed that the government should defend individuals rights, and socialists, who believed that the government should ensure equality by distributing wealth and power.

A group called the Soviets, workers and peasants led by Vladimir Lenin, opposed Kerensky's leadership. They believed that the provisional government represented only the interests of the middle class and the rich. Lenin and his followers formed a political party called the Bolsheviks, a Russian word meant to suggest that they represented a majority. By October, the Bolsheviks had overthrown the provisional government in an uprising that became known

Russian Tsar Nicholas II

as the October Revolution. The tsar, his family, and their servants were executed.

Russians with a variety of political beliefs, including Pavlov's son Victor, joined the White Army and took up arms against the Bolsheviks' Red Army. This civil war lasted from 1918–1920. The Red Army had seized most of the troops and supplies of the imperial army; they prevailed in this Russian civil war, which was almost as destructive to Russian life as World War I had been.[1]

Ivan Pavlov tried his best not to let these events disrupt his work. "What difference does a revolution make," he once asked, "when you have experiments to do in the laboratory?"[2] Nevertheless, he could not completely escape the personal, political, and economic consequences of world war, revolution, and civil war.

The country entered a time of miserable poverty. The newly established Bolshevik government could not stabilize the economy. The banking system collapsed, and Ivan Pavlov lost the money he had saved from his Nobel Prize award. To help feed themselves and the dogs, Ivan and the other workers in his laboratory had to grow their own vegetables on the lab's campus. Fortunately, Ivan had always enjoyed gardening. He found that physical labor provided a good balance for his hard intellectual toil.

"I cannot even compare the great satisfaction derived from manual labor with that obtained by mental effort, although I live all the time by the latter," Pavlov said. "This is obviously dependent on the fact that my grandfather himself plowed the soil."[3]

The Soviet form of government was based on communism, a system based on the ideas of German philosopher Karl Marx. This government did not completely follow Marx's teachings, though. Marx believed that workers should own the factories, mines, and other workplaces rather than holding jobs in companies owned by wealthy people. Under the Communist government of the Soviet Union, the state owned the factories, mines, and other workplaces and set pay for workers. Many workers and farmers, disliking the conditions set by the government, simply stopped working.

Harsh Government

The Bolsheviks were hostile to the formerly elite members of Russian society, including landowners, merchants and other business owners, and educated people. They were also suspicious of scholars, intellectuals, and members of the clergy. The Bolsheviks feared that such people might criticize their way of thinking and encourage other people to do the same. Under the new system of government, many politicians and people they liked received high pay. All other workers were paid less, whether they were factory workers, artists, teachers, or doctors. Academic posts were not awarded to the best students. Instead, they were given to people who let political notions influence their research.

Provisional Russian government leader, Aleksandr Kerensky.

Many people were arrested, killed, or labeled insane for verbalizing their disagreements with the government. Pavlov's son Victor was killed while in the White Army.[4]

Pavlov was outspoken and sometimes demanding in his dealings with the officials of the Soviet Union. He refused to accept the government-appointed scientists as his peers. When the Soviet commissar of education visited his laboratory, Pavlov would not let him in. Pavlov asked Lenin, now the head of the Soviet government, if he could move his laboratory to another country, somewhere where the living standards were higher. Lenin would not allow it. Pavlov wrote angry letters to Lenin about the way the government treated people who thought independently and spoke their minds. Despite Pavlov's defiant attitude, Lenin signed a decree recognizing Ivan Pavlov's "outstanding scientific service" on January 24, 1921.[5] The Soviet government doubled the Pavlov family's rations and poured money into building Pavlov special laboratory facilities.

Soviet leader Vladimir Lenin had a contentious relationship with his nation's most preeminent scientist, Ivan Pavlov. Despite this, Lenin recognized Pavlov's many achievements.

Lenin died in 1924, at which time Petrograd was named Leningrad in his honor. Pavlov's relationship with Joseph Stalin, Lenin's successor, was also hostile.

Still, Ivan Pavlov's fame protected him in a number of ways from being punished for his defiance. First, he stood as an example to the world of the brilliance of Soviet scientists. The Soviets held science in great esteem. As they saw it, their Marxist-Leninist politics were a sort of science, grounded in material reality rather than superstition, religion, or old-fashioned beliefs. Unfortunately, they encouraged scientists to replace honest investigations of fact with experiments whose results could be manipulated to support Marxist philosophy.

Second, Ivan Pavlov had friends and colleagues in many countries around the world. Those supporters would surely respond should Pavlov be persecuted. Ivan Pavlov and his son Vladimir traveled internationally to scientific conferences. Even though he was treated well, given a state official's salary rather than the smaller stipend of a scientist, he spoke out openly against the idea of Communism.

Pavlov Visits the United States

In 1923, he took a trip to the United States. He admired Americans, whom he saw as practical and hardworking as compared with the Russians of his time. The strain of the wars and turmoil, he believed, left many of his fellow countrymen feeling passive and overwhelmed. He was received as a dignitary at the Rockefeller Institute, where one of his former Military Medical Academy students was director of the biochemistry department. Vladimir Pavlov was his father's interpreter, as Ivan did not speak English. Pavlov was not prepared for the bustle of Grand Central Station in New York City. He was shaken down on a train platform by thieves, who stole the eight hundred dollars that the naive old man had in a visible bulge in his pocket.

It was during this visit that Pavlov said publicly he "would not sacrifice a frog's hind legs"[6] for the sake of what he believed was a

63

foolish experiment on the part of his country's leaders—the promotion of Communism worldwide. The United States, too, feared and mistrusted the Communists.

Ivan Pavlov left the Military Medical Academy in 1924. His resignation was a gesture of solidarity with other sons of priests who were being kicked out of the academy and other schools and being prevented from getting an education. He accepted the challenge of directing the newly established Institute of Physiology.

The Industrial Revolution had changed the way people worked all around the world. Pavlov combined some of the organizational structures of modern factories with the ethic of the traditional master-apprentice methods of teaching and learning. He was not an adept business

Pavlov's relationship with the Soviet government did not improve with the rise to power of Josef Stalin (above).

manager. Instead, he was known for his swift temper, occasional swearing, and controlling management style.

He was strict with his students because he was serious about his role as the master scientist. Ivan Pavlov did not believe that genius was responsible for his success. Instead, he gave credit for his accomplishments to his conscientiousness and strong work ethic. He hoped to inspire his students and other young people to cultivate the qualities needed for achievement in science—systematic rigor, passion, and modesty.[7]

Building a Legacy

BY THE LATE 1920S IVAN PAVLOV WAS admired by the Soviet government and by the scientific community around the world. He kept up his lifelong daily routine of days in the laboratory and nights in his study at home. His status gave him the freedom to devote more of his time to the exploration of the human mind. He continued to work at the Institute of Experimental Medicine in Leningrad, served as director of the new Institute of Physiology, and made regular visits to psychiatric hospitals.

New Investigations

Ivan Pavlov strongly defended his ideas about human and animal behavior against the new ideas of younger men. He tried to figure out how human language might have arisen from a chain of conditioned reflexes and to understand a type of mental disease called psychosis.

Studying conditioned reflexes in dogs had required special facilities free from distractions. To be absolutely sure of which stimulus was associated with a response, experimenters had to make sure that they could expose the dog to that stimulus by itself. The Institute of Experimental Medicine included "towers of silence" designed to keep the dog from receiving any stimulus other than the one being studied. The experimenter watched the dog through cameras and could introduce a stimulus, such as a particular sound, without the dog's seeing or smelling the researcher, hearing his footsteps as he approached, or being exposed to distractions from the outside world.

The isolation helped with the research, but the dogs often became anxious, sad, and confused by experiments in which food was withheld for long periods of time after a conditional stimulus was presented. Observing

A drawing of the exterior of Pavlov's Leningrad laboratory.

this, Pavlov became curious about how and why human beings suffer breakdowns. Russian physiologist Ivan Sechenov had said that the brain balances out too much "excitation" with "inhibition." Pavlov wondered whether that inhibition was the cause of mental patients' seeming to shut out reality.

In 1924, flooding in the coastal town of Leningrad, caused by a storm tide, created some interesting evidence for this hypothesis.

Floodwaters reached the dogs' feeding cages in the research lab, rising high enough to lift the animals to the ceilings of their pens. Because the cages were constructed with doors near the floor, rescuers had to pull the dogs' heads briefly underwater to pull them to safety.

These research dogs showed the same kind of behavior that human psychotics do. They lost the conditioning that experimenters had spent years instilling. Although most of the responses were relearned quickly, some dogs became skittish and fearful when confronted with strong stimuli, such as the loud ringing of an electric bell. Other dogs were terrified when the flooding was reenacted by experimenters running water across the floor. Certain dogs did not return to normal until they were moved to another building.[1]

Pavlov tried to apply theories about personality types to his dogs, identifying some as high-spirited and strong, others as sleepy, still others as whiny. He gave up. He concluded that every dog was unique and that he would

An artist's rendition of Pavlov attempting to save his dogs during a flood of the river Neva. The event altered the dogs' conditioned reflexes, which led Pavlov to a major breakthrough in his research.

probably never be able to find a number of categories small enough to manage.

When he saw his dogs' responses to the shock caused by the flood, Pavlov thought that the problem might be that the brain and nerves became so agitated that they could no longer carry out their job of inhibition. Perhaps, he reasoned, human mental patients experience the same thing. In visits with psychiatrists at

Russian hospitals, he advocated keeping mental patients in calm, quiet rooms, with minimal stimulation.

In Europe, other researchers were presenting new ideas about mental disease. For example, Sigmund Freud was writing about and teaching his theories of psychoanalysis. Freud and his students believed that human beings' behavior could be explained by conflict between the conscious mind (the desires, needs, likes, and dislikes that we know we have) and the unconscious mind (the fears, needs and desires that we have but are not aware of.)

The Birth of Behaviorism

In the United States, John Watson, Edward Thorndike, and, later, B. F. Skinner expanded on Pavlov's ideas about conditioning in an approach to psychology that is called behaviorism. The name comes from the theory's emphasis on behavior that can be observed, rather than on assumptions about what might be happening in the mind. American behaviorists made several important enhancements to Pavlov's theory.

Pavlov focused on "classical conditioning," the associations between stimuli and animals' involuntary physiological responses. John Watson tested this theory in the domain of human emotions. In his famous experiment with

The father of psychoanalysis, Sigmund Freud.

a child called Little Albert, Watson introduced an eleven-month-old boy to a white rat. Then he startled the child with a painfully loud noise. Little Albert became fearful when he saw the white rat. Eventually the boy would become afraid of anything he encountered that looked like a white rat.[2]

Edward Thorndike observed that animals repeat behaviors that lead to pleasurable experiences and avoid repeating actions that lead to unpleasant experiences.[3] B. F. Skinner built upon the notion of rewards and punishments. He was more interested in behaviors (things animals, including human beings, do) than he was in involuntary physiological or emotional responses. His writings describe how animals make associations between stimuli, behaviors they choose, and the consequences of those behaviors. Skinner used the term "operant conditioning" to indicate that the animals "operate," or act, on their environments.[4]

These behaviorists promoted the idea that behavioral psychologists could get both human beings and animals to do what they want them to do by using rewards and punishments. Their ideas are still used in education and child rearing. For instance, when teachers give out gold stars for good schoolwork or parents put children in time-out, they are applying the principles of operant conditioning.

In Pavlov's view, both the psychoanalysts and the behaviorists neglected what was most important. For him classical conditioning was not a way of understanding learning and behavior; it was a way to study the physiology of the brain, especially the cerebral cortex and the subcortical areas. So, he established weekly seminars, known as Pavlov's Wednesdays, to ensure that the students and assistants in his many laboratories stayed on track and were not distracted by other theories.[5]

At these meetings Ivan Pavlov would give a short statement. Then participants would have an informal discussion about their scientific work and ideas. Pavlov imposed a fine on students who used terminology from the world of psychology in their presentations. He demanded that they instead always refer to the structure of the brain and the mechanism of the nervous system. Sometimes he harshly criticized other well-known scientists. Because he was so respected in the scientific community, his

Harvard behavioral psychologist B. F. Skinner trains a small bird to perform specific tasks.

opinions occasionally showed up in the newspapers.

In a lecture series he gave in 1927, *Conditioned Reflexes,* Pavlov explained his conviction that physiologists, not psychologists, should take the lead in studying complex behavior. "In fact," he said, "it is still open to discussion whether psychology is a natural science, or whether it can be regarded as a science at all."[6]

Pavlov aimed to leave aside the questions of consciousness and individual personality. Nonetheless, he observed that his research dogs varied in their behavior and responses.

Pavlov's Final Years

In 1926, Pavlov was seventy-seven years old. In the last few months of the year, he developed a serious illness. He had stomach pains, fever, and chills. He also developed jaundice. (The whites of his eyes became yellow.) Jaundice is usually a symptom of liver disease. Sara feared the worst—that her husband had liver cancer. Ivan

Pavlov was also afraid. He tried to convince himself that he had a disease that was less likely to be fatal: malaria, a contagious infection sometimes spread by mosquito bites. Finally doctors diagnosed a problem with his digestive system. He had gallstones, which are hard clusters of cholesterol, bile salts, and calcium.

When the Congress of Russian Scientists met in Leningrad, a number of surgeons visited him. Pavlov asked a professor he met at a conference to perform surgery. It was a success. One of the assisting surgeons presented Sara with a large stone that had been removed from Pavlov's common bile duct.

On August 27, 1927, Pavlov wrote to his friend and associate Boris Petrovich Babkin, from Karlsbad, where he had gone to recuperate: "The operation has freed me in a marvelous way from all symptoms of illness: two weeks after it I was completely well. This astonishing fact is one more proof of the law that the organism should be treated like a machine. Exactly like a speck of dust in a watch!—The

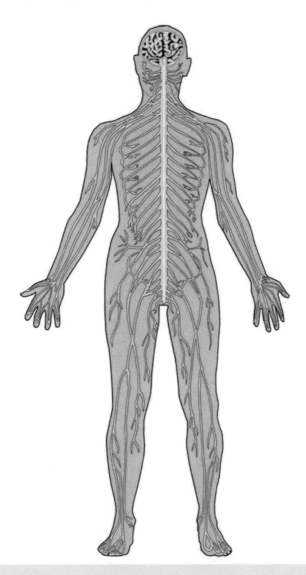

A diagram outlining the human nervous system. Pavlov believed that the central nervous system controlled all other systems of the body.

stone was removed and the machine resumed its normal functions!"[7] He told Babkin that he was strong and healthy again and was ready to return to work.

Ivan Pavlov was strong enough in 1929 to make a second trip to the United States. Just a week before his eightieth birthday, Pavlov attended the Ninth International Congress of the International Psychological Association, held at Yale University in Connecticut. He addressed the assembled psychologists in Russian, through a translator.[8]

By the summer of 1935, Ivan Pavlov was eighty-five years old. He continued to conduct research and attend conferences but delegated more and more of his work to his much-younger students. He developed an infection that affected his entire body. His students worried that he might be dying. As much as he could, Ivan Pavlov kept up the disciplined lifestyle he had learned from his godfather and maintained with the help of his wife. The year was a hard one. Sara suffered from heart problems. Right before Christmas, the family learned that Ivan's youngest son, Vsevolod, had inoperable pancreatic cancer. Vsevolod died before the year ended. He was only forty years old and left behind a widow.

In February 1936, Ivan Pavlov contracted a bad case of the flu. He went to work as usual on February 21 and, according to his wife's report, enjoyed a pancake dinner. The next day, he was too sick to work. His temperature rose. He developed bronchitis, and then pneumonia. On February 26, 1936, Pavlov spoke with his granddaughters, inviting them to visit the following Sunday, the first of March. On February 27, at 2:52 A.M., Ivan Pavlov squeezed his wife's hand and died. He was buried on March 1, after lying in state in Leningrad.

The Soviet Union honored its native son in many ways. They paid for his funeral. They installed a monument to him in Leningrad's central square. They turned his study at the Institute of Experimental Medicine into a museum. They arranged a pension for his widow (until her death in 1947), and renamed the First Leningrad Medical Institute in his honor. His brain was preserved at the Brain Institute of Moscow.[9]

Throughout his life Ivan Pavlov devoted himself to the belief in science, which drew him away from his religious career. In his tireless effort to understand the truths of the human body, he changed the way we understand the mind, the brain, and the digestive system. He reinvented the process of scientific research itself.

Ivan Pavlov said of scientific work, "Gradualness, gradualness, and gradualness. From the very beginning of your work, school yourself to severe gradualness in the accumulation of knowledge."[10] Decades after his death, his words still ring true. For example, in Pavlov's time there was a heated debate. Some theorists, like Pavlov, said that the central nervous system controlled the various systems of the body. Others believed systems regulated themselves with chemicals. It turns out that they were all correct.

Pavlov's discoveries about the vagus nerve established that the central nervous system indeed plays a role in digestion. In 1902, William Bayliss and Everett Starling, two English scientists, discovered secretin, which regulates the acidity of the intestinal tract. They created the term "hormone" to describe chemicals like secretin that have physiological effects. When he learned about their work, Pavlov remarked, "Of course they are right. It is clear that we did not take out an exclusive patent for the discovery of truth."[11]

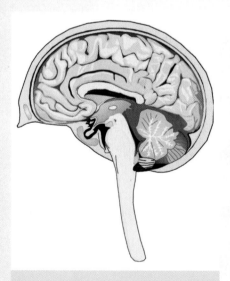

A cutaway illustration showing the interior of the human brain.

Modern specialists called neuroendocrinologists study how the brain regulates different organs. They say that one of the things the vagus nerve does is to tell the cells to release chemicals. Those chemicals, the hormones, actually regulate the secretion of the digestive juices.

As a young man, Ivan Pavlov left the religious profession, but he never abandoned his priestly humility before the uncertainties of life. Pavlov also never forgot those who made his accomplishments possible. In his autobiographical writing, Ivan thanked his wife for attending to the details of the family's day-to-day life so that he could focus on his work.

The museum at the Institute of Experimental Medicine displays tokens of his gratitude, too. The room that was Pavlov's private study looks today the way it did when he retreated to it with his notebooks and his mugs of tea. A photograph of his mentor, Carl Ludwig, hangs above the writing desk. In the garden is a more formal tribute, a sculpted fountain Pavlov commissioned and approved in the final year of his life. It is a monument to the dog.[12]

History Has Its Say

MOST STUDENTS FIRST ENCOUNTER THE work of Ivan Pavlov in their introductory psychology courses, not in their science classes. Just as history shaped the way Pavlov worked during his life, it influenced the way that the world received his work, and continues to define his legacy.

During the first half of the twentieth century, people became increasingly interested in developing a science that could explain the human mind. In the mid-nineteenth century, still photography, a relatively new technology, brought to the public in many countries, especially in the United States, the first documentary images of the horrors of war. The technology for moving pictures was developed about the same time that World War I occurred. By the end of World War II in 1945, civilians saw footage of Allied soldiers in Germany as they discovered prisoners in concentration camps. Millions of people had been imprisoned, systematically tortured, and killed.

People around the world tried to make sense of the human behavior they had witnessed. Psychologists offered a scientific way to explore the topic and soon joined religious leaders, writers, and politicians as authorities on the human condition.

Pavlov's research on the higher nervous activity led psychologists and physiologists of his time to a new understanding of how the different sections of the brain work. It laid the groundwork for entirely new ways of studying and theorizing about learning, behavior, personality, intelligence, mental illness, and brain injuries and diseases.

Also, many of Pavlov's criticisms of the strict behaviorists, the psychoanalysts who followed the teachings of Freud, and the zoo

The scene at a Nazi death camp—grim evidence of the systematic torture and murder perpetrated by the Nazis. In the wake of the Holocaust, the desire to understand human behavior grew even stronger.

psychologists have been vindicated. In 1921, Otto Loewi of Austria discovered a class of chemicals now called the neurotransmitters, chemicals that transmit nerve impulses.[1] That and other discoveries have led to a twenty-first-century science of psychology in which neurologists, cognitive psychologists, and psychiatrists—like Pavlov's Wednesdays seminar students—must account for the known facts about physiology of the brain in their theories and in the treatments they propose.

Consumer Culture

The advent of consumer culture and advertising also bears Pavlov's mark. John Watson was an American admirer of Pavlov's, who coined the term "behaviorism," After years of study based on Pavlov's work at Johns Hopkins University he embarked on a second career—working for the advertising firm J. Walter Thompson.[2]

Watson applied the lessons he had learned in the laboratory to his work in advertising. He believed that when people see photographs of juicy hamburgers, their mouths will water, and when they see images of models with

In 1921, Austrian scientist Otto Loewi discovered a class of chemicals known today as neurotransmitters.

Modern commercials and advertising still often use the Pavlov's principals of conditioning to get the public to purchase their products.

shiny white teeth, they will feel their hearts race with anxiety about the appearance of their own teeth. Then they will attempt to satisfy their hunger by buying the burger or ease their social fears by purchasing the toothpaste mentioned in the ad.

One hundred years after Pavlov first announced his intention to study conditioned responses, the creators of advertisements for television, radio, billboards, the world wide web and magazines assume that human beings are more similar to Pavlov's dogs than they are different.

Activities

Classical conditioning refers to involuntary physiological responses to stimuli such as salivation and sweating. When the doctor hits your knee with his hammer, he is testing for the patellar reflex.

The theory of behaviorism extended the principles of classical conditioning to apply to voluntary behavior. A stimulus triggers a reflex, and the animal's motor responses (movement) supply more stimuli. Behaviorists believe that all behavior can be traced to a long series of stimuli and responses.

▶ **Activity 1: PET BEHAVIOR**
If your family or a friend has a pet dog, cat, bird, or fish, you can observe conditioned behavior. In fact, you have probably noticed it already.

- What does the dog or cat do when a family member opens a can with a can opener?
- Shake a dog's or cat's bag of kibble. How does the pet respond?
- What do aquarium fish do when a person approaches?
- Watch dogs in their homes, or in a local park. Do they follow word commands, such as "sit" and "come"? Do they respond to visual stimuli— such as the shaking of a leash or toy, and to noises, such as whistling?

▶ **Activity 2: CLICKER TRAINING**

For this activity you will need a partner and a clicker, a small plastic device with a flap of metal attached inside a hole that fits your finger. When you press and release that metal flap, it makes a loud clicking noise. You can find this item in a pet store. It is sometimes used in training dogs through operant conditioning.

The behaviorist in the experiment will use the clicker to get the subject to perform a simple behavior (something like sitting down in a particular chair or touching a certain object in the room).

- Decide what you want your friend to do, but don't say what it is.
- Instruct your friend to begin.
- When the subject moves in the right direction, click your clicker. The clicker is a "consequence" for doing something right.

Keep clicking every time your subject gets closer to doing what you want. Eventually your friend will stumble onto the correct behavior.

If you have a pet dog, you can use the clicker to teach your dog tricks. To do this, first do what Pavlov did—click the clicker and give your dog a treat. Soon the dog will learn that click equals treat.

Chronology

1849—Ivan Petrovich Pavlov is born in Ryazan, Russia, on September 14. He is the first child of Peter Pavlov, a village priest, and Varvara Pavlova, the daughter of a priest.

1870—Enrolls in the St. Petersburg University to study physics and mathematics.

1873—Begins collaborating on a study of the physiology of the pancreatic nerves.

1875—Graduates from the St. Petersburg University with the degree of Candidate of Natural Science and enrolls as a student at the Military Medical Academy.

1879—Graduates from the Military Medical Academy.

1880—Proposes to Seraphima (Sara) Vasilievna Karchevskaya on June 13; begins postgraduate studies at the Military Medical Academy.

1881—Ivan and Sara marry on May 1. They have five children—sons Wirchik (who dies in early childhood), Vladimir, Vsevolod, Victor, and one daughter Vera.

1883—Submits a thesis on the nerves of the heart; earns Doctor of Medicine degree.

1884—Appointed to position of lecturer in physiology at the Military Medical Academy.

1885–86—Studies abroad.

1888–90—Works in Sergei Botkin's laboratory.

1890—Appointed professor of pharmacology at the Military Medical Academy.

1891—Appointed to the position of Director of the Department of Physiology in the Institute of Experimental Medicine.

1895—Appointed to chair of the physiology department.

1897—Publishes *Lectures on the Functions of the Principal Digestive Glands*.

1901—Elected as a corresponding member of the Russian Academy of Sciences.

1903—Delivers a talk at the Fourteenth International Medical Congress in Madrid; introduces his discovery of the conditioned reflexes, the new intellectual passion to which he will devote the rest of his career.

1904—Receives Nobel Prize in Physiology or Medicine for work on the physiology of the digestive gland; talks about the conditioned reflexes in his award speech.

1907—Elected Academician of the Russian Academy of Sciences.

1912—Cambridge University in England grants Pavlov an honorary doctorate.

1917—The Russian Revolution throws the tsars out of power and installs the government that will become the Soviet Union. Although the Soviet government persecutes many scientists, they allow Pavlov to continue his work.

1921—Vladimir Lenin signs a decree that recognizes "the outstanding scientific services of Academician I. P. Pavlov, which are of enormous significance to the working class of the whole world."

1924—Pavlov resigns from professorship at the Military Medical Academy and accepts the position of director at the newly established Institute of Physiology.

1925—Pavlov nominated for the Nobel Prize in Physiology or Medicine for his work on conditioned responses, the central nervous system, and higher nerve activity; he does not win.

1927—Pavlov nominated for the Nobel Prize in Physiology or Medicine; again, he does not win.

1927—Pavlov establishes Wednesday seminars, known as Pavlov's Wednesdays, to discuss work in progress; notes from the discussions are published throughout the world.

1929—Pavlov nominated a final time for the Nobel Prize in Physiology or Medicine; again, he does not win.

1935—Vsevolod, Pavlov's youngest son, dies of pancreatic cancer.

1935—Soviet government builds a laboratory for Pavlov; facilities include isolated rooms where experimenters can control dogs' exposure to light, sound, and scents.

1936—On February 27, Ivan Petrovich Pavlov dies in Leningrad at age eighty-six. Thousands of people see him lying in state. People buy tickets to the March 1 funeral. He is buried with Vsevolod.

Chapter Notes

Chapter 1. The Mastermind

1. Daniel Phillip Todes, "From the Machine to the Ghost Within: Pavlov's Transition from Digestive Physiology to Conditional Reflexes," *American Psychologist*, vol. 52, 1997, pp. 947–955.

2. B.P. Babkin, *Pavlov: A Biography*, (Chicago: University of Chicago Press, 1949), p. 62.

3. Ibid., p. 122.

4. Daniel Phillip Todes, *Pavlov's Physiology Factory: Experiment, Interpretation, Laboratory Enterprise*, (Baltimore: Johns Hopkins University Press, 2001), p. 131.

5. Ibid., p. 194.

6. Babkin, p. 79.

7. "The Nobel Prize in Physiology or Medicine 1904," *Nobelprize.org*, April 11, 2005, <http://nobelprize.org/medicine/laureates/1904/index.html> (September 29, 2005).

Chapter 2. Pavlov's Calling

1. B.P. Babkin, *Pavlov: A Biography*, (Chicago: University of Chicago Press, 1949), p. 8.

2. Ibid., pp. 5–11.

Chapter 3. Studying Natural Sciences

1. B.P. Babkin, *Pavlov: A Biography*, (Chicago: University of Chicago Press, 1949), p. 286.

2. Ibid., p. 23.

Chapter 4. The Courtship of Seraphima

1. B.P. Babkin, *Pavlov: A Biography*, (Chicago: University of Chicago Press, 1949), p. 37.

2. Y.P. Frolvov, *Pavlov and His School*, trans. C.P. Dutt, (1938; rep., New York: Johnson Reprint Corporation, 1970), pp. 264–265.

3. Babkin, p. 13 and p. 134.

4. "Ivan Pavlov," *Wikipedia*, September 28, 2005, <http://en.wikipedia.org/wiki/Ivan_Pavlov> (September 29, 2005).

5. Mayer Resnick, "Putting 'Physiology' into the Nobel Prize: 2004 Marks 100th Anniversary of Pavlov's Award," *American Physiology Society*, October 6, 2004, <http://www.the-aps.org/press/journal/04/29.htm> (September 29, 2005).

Chapter 5. The Theory of the Conditioned Reflex

1. Daniel Phillip Todes, "From the Machine to the Ghost Within: Pavlov's Transition from Digestive Physiology to Conditional Reflexes," *American Psychologist*, vol. 52, 1997, pp. 947–955.

2. Ibid., pp. 947–955.

3. B.P. Babkin, *Pavlov: A Biography* (Chicago: University of Chicago Press, 1949), pp. 311–316.

4. Pavlov's Nobel lecture, <http://nobelprize .org/medicine/laureates/1904/pavlovlecture.html> (November 29, 2005).

Chapter 6. Ivan Pavlov's Russia

1. "World War I," *Wikipedia*, September 29, 2005, <http://en.wikipedia.org/wiki/World_ War_I> (September 29, 2005).

2. W. Horsley Gantt, "Pavlov, Ivan Petrovich," *Britannica Guide to the Nobel Prizes*, 1997, Encyclopedia Britannica, Inc., <http://www. britannica.com/nobel/micro/455_62.html> (September 29, 2005).

3. Y.P. Frolvov, *Pavlov and His School*, trans. C.P. Dutt, (1938; repr., New York: Johnson Reprint Corporation, 1970), p. 252.

4. "Ivan Pavlov" *Wikipedia*, September 29, 2005, <http://en.wikipedia.org/wiki/Ivan_Pavlov> (September 29, 2005).

5. "Ivan Pavlov—Biography," *Nobelprize.org*, April 11, 2005, <http://nobelprize.org/medicine/ laureates/1904/pavlov-bio.html> (September 29, 2005).

6. Gantt, "Pavlov, Ivan Petrovich," *Britannica Guide to the Nobel Prizes*.

7. B.P. Babkin, *Pavlov: A Biography*, (Chicago: University of Chicago Press, 1949), p. 110.

Chapter 7. Building a Legacy

1. Y.P. Frolvov, *Pavlov and His School*, trans. C.P. Dutt, (1938, repr., Johnson Reprint Corporation, 1970), pp. 214–216.

2. "B.F. Skinner," *Wikipedia*, September 28, 2005, <http://en.wikipedia.org/wiki/B._F._Skinner> (September 29, 2005).

3. Wikipedia, "Edward Thorndike," June 3, 2005, <http://en.wikipedia.org/wiki/Edward_ Thorndike> (September 29, 2005)

4. "John B. Watson," *Wikipedia*, September 28, 2005, <http://en.wikipedia.org/wiki/John_Watson> (September 29, 2005).

5. Frolov, p. 262.

6. Ivan Pavlov, "Conditioned Reflexes: An Investigation of the Physiological Activity of the Cerebral Cortex, 1927," tran. G.V. Anrep, *Classics in the History of Psychology*, <http://psychclassics. yorku.ca/Pavlov/> (September 29, 2005).

7. B.P. Babkin, *Pavlov: A Biography*, (Chicago: University of Chicago Press, 1949), p. 176.

8. John D. Hogan, Ph.D., "The Founding of Psi Chi at the Ninth International Congress of Psychology," *National Honor Society in Psychology*, September 3, 1999, <http://www.psichi.org/about/ history/history_3.asp> (September 30, 2005).

9. Babkin, p. 229.

10. "Quotations by Category: Beginnings," *Deepbox.com*, 2003–2004, <http://www.deepbox.com/ categories/Beginnings/40.html> (September 30, 2005).

11. John Henderson, "Ernest Starling and 'Hormones': an Historical Commentary," *Journal of Endocrinology*, 2005, v. 184, pp. 5–10, <http:// joe.endocrinology-journals.org/cgi/content/ full/184/1/5> (November 29, 2005).

12. "The Monument to a Dog," The Institute of Experimental Medicine, n.d., <http://www. iemrams.spb.ru:8101/english/dog-monum.htm> (September 29, 2005).

Chapter 8. History Has Its Say

1. "The Nobel Prize in Physiology or Medicine 1936," April 14, 2005, <http://nobelprize.org/medicine/laureates/1936/index.html> (September 29, 2005).

2. "John B. Watson," *Wikipedia*, September 28, 2005, <http://en.wikipedia.org/wiki/John_Watson> (September 29, 2005).

Glossary

Russian History and Culture Terms

Allied powers—Countries that came together against Germany and the Axis powers in World War I, including the United States, Great Britain, and the Soviet Union.

Bolshevik—Derived from a Russian word meaning "majority," the Bolsheviks claimed to represent peasants and workers. They forcibly took over the government of Russia and established what would become the Union of Soviet Socialist Republics (U. S. S. R), or the Soviet Union.

gorodki—A Russian game similar to croquet.

"Great War"—This war, which began in 1914, eventually included almost all of Europe, as well as the United States and Japan. It was known as the War to End All Wars until another war broke out in 1939, involving most of the same countries. The Great War is now usually called World War I, and the 1939 war is called World War II.

praktikanty—Young medical students in turn-of-the-century Russia.

Russian Civil War (1918–1920)—Conflict between the government that took over after the Russian Revolution and those who opposed that government, primarily members of the middle and upper classes.

Russian Revolution of 1917—Uprising which resulted in the end of Russia's Imperial era led by tsars, who inherited power, and the establishment of the Soviet Union.

Soviet Union—A Communist-led country that became one of two world superpowers. (The other was the United States.) Until 1991, the Soviet Union exercised control over most of the Eastern European countries. As of 2005, most of the former Soviet regions are loosely organized into the Commonwealth of Independent States.

Classical Conditioning Terms

conditional (conditioned) response—Reflex reaction to a formerly neutral stimulus that has been associated with an unconditional stimulus such as food.

conditional (conditioned) stimulus—Stimulus that generates a response in an animal after it is paired with something that is naturally stimulating.

excitation—In the theory Pavlov inherited from Sechenov, the "turning on" of a region of the central nervous system in response to stimuli from the environment.

extinction—Loss of a conditioned response when the conditioned stimulus is presented repeatedly without being followed by the unconditioned stimulus.

inhibition—In the theory Pavlov inherited from Sechenov, "turning off" of a region of the central nervous system in compensation for overstimulation.

reflex—Set of automatic, involuntary physiological activities.

response—The reaction to a stimulus.

stimulus—Something an animal perceives through the senses and then responds to.

stimulus discrimination—Response only to stimuli similar to the conditioned one; for instance, a dog who has been conditioned to salivate in response to hearing his master's keys jingle might not give the same response to the jingling of another person's key ring with a different sound.

stimulus generalization—Association of a conditioned response with a stimulus that is similar but not identical to another conditioned stimulus.

unconditional (unconditioned) response—Reflex that happens in response to something in the environment that doesn't have to be learned (for example, when hungry dogs or human beings see or smell food, their mouths water).

unconditional (unconditioned) stimulus—Something in the environment that causes a response in the body that doesn't have to be learned (for example, the sight or scent of food).

Psychological Terms

behaviorism—An approach to psychology that emphasizes observable behavior.

cognitive psychology—An approach to psychology that emphasizes mental processes.

neurosis—A kind of mental disorder in which a person is anxious, depressed, or manic (overstimulated) but still knows what is real. (This term is no longer used by psychologists.)

psychoanalysis—An approach to psychology that emphasizes early childhood experiences and the influence of thoughts and feelings that a person is not aware of.

psychosis—A kind of mental disorder in which a person loses contact with reality. (The person sees things that don't exist, or has bizarre ideas.)

Physiological Terms

alimentary canal—Pathway that carries food from the mouth, through the esophagus, stomach, and intestines, and finally out of the body as waste.

cancer—Disease characterized by an overgrowth of cells.

common bile duct—Opening that connects the lower intestine and the liver.

cerebral cortex—Outer layer of the brain, made up of two parts: one part controls the five senses, the other controls movement.

gastric—Relating to the stomach.

hormone—Chemical produced in one part of the body and carried through the bloodstream to other organs, where it has some affect on their functions. Insulin, estrogen, and testosterone are hormones.

neurotransmitters—Naturally occurring chemicals in the brain that are responsible for communication among nerve cells. Serotonin, epinephrine, and histamine are neurotransmitters.

pancreas—Organ in the abdomen that secretes digestive enzymes and hormones that allow the body to metabolize (break down) sugars, fats, and proteins.

patella—The kneecap.

secretin—A hormone found in the abdominal organs of the digestive system. It regulates the level of acidity in those organs.

vagus nerve—A large nerve that conducts signals from the cranium, through the heart, and all the way to the colon. It helps to regulate heartbeat and blood pressure, as well as digestion.

vivisection—Operation done on a living animal for purposes of experimentation.

General Science Terms

acute experiment—Experiment on a live animal in which an experimenter gathers data on a one-time basis, such as during an operation.

chronic experiment—Experiment on a live animal in which an experimenter gathers data by watching the animal over time.

empirical—Based on direct observation or experience.

experiment—An investigation or test set up to confirm or disprove a hypothesis or to support or discredit a theory.

esophagus—Part of the alimentary canal that contracts to force swallowed food from the throat down into the stomach.

fistula—Abnormal connection from an organ, intestine, or vessel to some other part of the body or to the outside of the body.

hypothesis—Proposed explanation of something that has been observed; often, a hypothesis can be tested through an experiment or study.

Pavlov pouch—Pocket created surgically to isolate a part of an organ such as the stomach or pancreas, allowing it to function normally and be available for observation and collection of secretions. Ivan Pavlov was the first surgeon to master this technique, which is still used in the early twenty-first century.

Pavlov sling—Device that holds research dogs in a still and relatively comfortable position during some laboratory experiments.

study—The use of experiments or other fact-gathering methods to investigate a complex question.

theory—Well-developed, systematic explanation of a number of facts.

Further Reading

Books

Bankston, John. *Sigmund Freud: Exploring the Mysteries of the Mind*. Berkeley Heights, N.J.: Enslow Publishers, Inc., 2006.

Todes, Daniel Philip. *Ivan Pavlov: Exploring the Animal Machine*. New York: Oxford University Press, 2000.

Todes, Daniel P. *Pavlov's Physiology Factory: Experiment, Interpretation, Laboratory Enterprise*. Baltimore: Johns Hopkins University Press, 2001.

Internet Addresses

Ivan Pavlov

http://www.ivanpavlov.com/

A Science Odyssey: People and Discoveries: Ivan Pavlov

http://www.pbs.org/wgbh/aso/databank/entries/bhpavl.html

Ivan Pavlov—Biography

http://nobelprize.org/medicine/laureates/1904/pavlov-bio.html

Index